Killing Lean

Leadership Behaviors, Policies and Practices that Kill Lean efforts

By

Joe D'Apollonio II

Specific Examples that can help you make changes **TODAY** to propel your lean efforts **TOMORROW**.

Copyright ©2021 Joseph D'Apollonio II

All rights reserved

The examples outlined in this book are based on my personal observation and interpretation. The actual intent by the person observed may have been different. Some pronouns have been changed for diversity reasons. The sequence of examples does not match my work history in any way.

No part of this book may be reproduced, or stored in a retrieval system, or transmitted in any form or by any means, electronic, mechanical, photocopying, recording, or otherwise, without express written permission of the publisher.

ISBN-10: 9798707116452

Cover design by: Dawn D'Apollonio

Printed in the United States of America

Thank You

A special thanks to my wife **Dawn** for giving me the time during a difficult transition to dedicate to this book. It's not easy dealing with an unemployment event and spending time away from actively looking for our next opportunity made it a little more nerve racking. Thank you for the space and the time. It was a great stress relief for me. I love you always and forever.

I would also like to thank **Will Wilberscheid** who made some notable enhancements to the book and who has challenged me to become a better lean leader over the last year and a half. His drive to put respect for people at the forefront of every conversation was a blessing for me in a difficult situation and his forward to this book is a credit to his foundational understanding of lean. This book is better because of his input.

Foreword

By Will Wilbersheid

"The Toyota style is not to create results by working hard. It is a system that says there is no limit to people's creativity. People don't go to Toyota to 'work' they go there to 'think'."
Taiichi Ohno

Lean starts and ends with a respect for people. On that front, Joe D'Apollonio and I are in full agreement. We both subscribe to Taiichi Ohno and the way he viewed people as the cornerstone for any real lean transformation. Go to where the work happens and ask the people doing the work how to get better. But you better pack a lunch. Because believe me, they will tell you. (Bring lots of pen and paper).

As a Lean Six Sigma Black Belt, I have had the opportunity to be a part of lean transformations in remanufacturing, logistics, front-office, call centers, and now in transactional spaces. I say transformation because it is a major shift in culture and mindset.

People are addicted to their piles of stuff. Whether parts, data, emails, pallets, you name it. The story never changes. Lean is great and all but if can never work in THIS space. We are too technical. Too specialized. Too variable. What we do is an art not a science. Lean is for manufacturing. That car stuff won't work here. And yet somehow it always works.

Joe brought me into an enormous, complicated lean system spanning many countries and business disciplines.

Each of the centers were at different starting points in their lean evolutions. It was so overwhelming it was hard to know where to start. But in his calm, confident manner, Joe said, "It all starts with respect for people. Just go talk to 'em." And so I did. Joe has a subtle art of making the complicated simple. And reminding us all to lean into our tools (no pun intended) and stick to the basics. They are called "the classics" for a reason.

The danger of any lean journey is not the launch. Launches are exciting. There are bottles of champagne. Big, flowery speeches. People are fired up and deeply committed to the process. There are even tears. Aaaaaand then a year goes by. It isn't new or exciting anymore. People realize that change is difficult. And respecting people is a whole lot harder than everyone thought. (Wait a minute. I have to ask them their opinion AND let them be a part of the solution???)

Joe wrote this book, in part, to call out the dangers of why many lean journeys stall. Or fail altogether. Joe has seen lean executed in massive manufacturing centers at an elite level. Across incredibly complex business models. And even in the US Navy. Leaders pick and choose the bits of lean that they like. But they throw out the parts that do not align. (We love problem solving and big fancy charts so everyone has to do that for sure. But we don't like employee criticism at the daily management boards. And we darn sure don't want our team members to stop working and be part of kaizen bursts. So we won't encourage those bits.)

I read this simple call to action and found myself guilty of several of the mistakes called out here. We all fall into traps. Based on ego. Or our previous experience. Sometimes our thinking gets clouded. Luckily, there are guys like Joe, who are patient, kind and will call us back to center and remind us why we are on this journey. Why we dedicated out lives to problem solving and crushing waste like the deadly enemy that it is.

Waste is the enemy. Not team members who tell us that our system stinks. Real, measurable savings are our friend. Not a bunch of "lean wallpaper" that looks great but drives no value. So, thanks for the call to action, Joe. Respect for people never goes out of style.

Will Wilberscheid, LSSBB

Destroyer of Waste; Passionate People Advocate

Table of Contents

1. Level Setting - 9

2. Leaving Your Sales Processes Untouched - 13

3. Creating KPI's For "Lean" - 23

4. Giving Senior Leaders Too Much Time To Get It - 33

5. Turning Lean Into A Checklist - 41

6. Misunderstanding the Basic Concepts of Lean - 49

7. The Rest of the Top Ten - 61

8. Meet Will Wilberscheid – 83

1 – Level Setting

First, Thank You for taking the time to read this book. I greatly appreciate it and I sincerely hope you take away a few key learnings to apply in your work.

I decided to write this book for two reasons; First, my profound belief in the Respect for People and second, because I was tired of hearing and reading about "lean failures". I was especially tired of reading about them as if "lean" was the reason for the failure.

Respect for people is the foundation for lean. Anything less than this is disrespectful in my opinion. I am tired of seeing this disrespect. I am tired of seeing the negative effects of these behaviors on the people on your teams. They are the ones who suffer. They are the ones who work longer hours to meet irrational deadlines. They are the ones who spend countless hours preparing fancy reports for you to skim through and delete within minutes. They are the ones who see you staying the same while they are told to completely change everything they learned in the past 2,4 or 10 years. They are the ones I feel sorry for and they are the ones that I hope will experience some positive changes soon.

On top of my concern for the hard workers on your teams, I wrote this book to give you some clear and specific areas to focus your improvement activity on. To be honest, I have read hundreds of articles and several books about "lean failures" and other issues with lean implementations. Each of them has merit, but I never found any that were specific enough and open enough to give you something you can act on. I hope these short chapters make it easy to read and will be a quick reference guide for you as you move forward in your lean journey. If you have not started your lean journey, I hope you learn from a few mistakes that I have seen over the years. Ones that are done with the best of intentions, but always seem to have the opposite effect on the team.

With that said, please allow me to be blunt and matter-of-fact when I outline the top behaviors, policies and practices I have observed, first hand, that have significantly hindered the lean efforts in businesses across the globe. It doesn't do anyone any good to sugar coat the truth, so I will not be doing that on these pages. Since you made the choice to read this book, I will make the assumption that you are interested in hearing some observations and are open to making a few changes to the way you approach this thing called lean.

I have been working in the lean space for over twenty years. Much less than some of the great mentors and leader's we have all learned so much from, but enough to see and hear the common themes that hinder progress and lead to failure in lean efforts. The more I see and hear, the more common the story.

You might be asking yourself, why does this guy think he knows the answers? That would be a fair question. I don't claim to be the world's lean czar with all the answers. What I do claim is that I have been in the break room, on the shop floor, in the conference room after the meeting, in the hallways and in the masses as they walk back to their cubes from town halls. Meaning, I have been where the real conversations happen.

The positions I have held put me smack in the middle of lean transformations, but not at the VP level where people shy away from unloading the truth. Yes, people don't tell you the real story. I don't know why. Maybe they tried a hundred times and you ignored them each time. Maybe they think it won't matter and maybe they just figure that you are too busy to listen.

The bottom line is I have heard it all and I have even tried to support your actions many times in an effort to change their minds. But time and time again, senior leaders keep repeating the actions and the opinions and actions they produce are all the same. No matter what function, no matter how small the team or how large the company, the same story plays out.

In addition to the common story, I noticed the common silence when it comes to the issues I was observing. The Lean community rarely talks about the specifics and the rest of the business community just finds excuses for "lean failures".

Failure was always directed at "senior leadership", but no one was telling them exactly what they were doing (or not doing) that was causing the issues. So, after ten years, I have said enough is enough. The following six chapters are the blunt realities of what "you" are doing that is killing your lean efforts.

2 - Leaving Your Sales Processes Untouched

The biggest elephant in the room is indeed Sales processes. Yes, some companies have dabbled in some aspects of the sales processes, but the vast majority have steered clear of bringing "Lean" into the sales arena. HUGE MISTAKE.

I hear the roar now; Sales is an art. Sales is not a process. Sales is too important to mess with. Excuses, Excuses, Excuses! That is all this is. Let me be clear, this is not the sales team's fault; they are part of the problem, but the main responsibility lies with the senior leaders of the company. They are the ones who have ultimately made the decision to avoid the golden processes. They are the ones who have decided to let the sales team do what the sales team does.

So why is this a killer to Lean? Because the sales processes affect nearly every other process in the company! It does not matter how big or small your company is, your sales processes DRIVE your business processes. And these very same processes are the ones that drive an estimated 80% of the waste in the company. Think about that. You have processes that are creating nearly 80% of the overall waste in your company ...... and you allow them to continue with no true lean efforts. Yes, the 80% is my personal estimate, but I have developed that estimate by evaluating end-to-end process performance in several companies over the last twenty years. I have worked in manufacturing and have engaged in nearly every other non-manufacturing process there is, except Sales. So, I have developed that estimate the hard way. I have had to deal with it most of my career. And, I actually think this is a conservative estimate. Let me give a few examples of what I mean.

First, most sales teams are compensated by some type of bonus structure. This structure provides them with the highest take home pay when they land the highest deals. That makes sense. You can't argue with the logic – the company wins big, so the salesperson is rewarded accordingly. The problem with this is that most of those structures have time frames for the bonuses. Some are monthly. Some are quarterly and some are other. And most of them have limits for each month or quarter and other. So, what behavior does this drive within the salespeople? Well, data and history show that the sales people max out their "personal" account. After all, they are human beings and most human beings would logically learn the pay structure and then figure out how they can maximize their take home pay within the directed structure.

Here are some common sales behaviors. If I have met my monthly max, then I will hold the next order until next month. If I am just under my maximum payout going into the final week then I will shave off a little off the price to "make the sale". And if I am close to knocking it out of the park, I will keep it a secret until I am 100% sure I have secured the deal. These are natural behaviors. This is not unethical or unprofessional or any other "wrong" label. This is the actions and behaviors that senior leaders create with their current sales compensation plans. Please do not act like I am making assumptions or exaggerating – if you are thinking that then your ears are not open. You are making the same mistakes that have been plaguing organizations for the past fifty years and you are fostering the havoc that these behaviors cause within the organization. What havoc you might ask. Well, let's discuss a few.

For the case where the person holds off placing the order until the following week (aka month), there is a failure to level load the production schedule. They have just incorporated a pattern that is not natural to the process. They have changed the process and thus they have injected variation into all the downstream processes. Procurement will see an abnormal order, operations will feel a spike, logistics will be beyond capacity and invoicing will be sporadic. These are just a few examples. All of this will end up having a negative impact on accounts receivables.

Moving on to the push to meet their maximum payout. The hockey stick has been used as a visual for many sales curves. The reason is that sales start off slow and then skyrocket towards the end of the cycle. This has been talked about for years. And the fact is IT IS TRUE. This is exactly what happens month after month and quarter after quarter. And senior leadership allows it to happen. By letting it happen, you are forcing the quoting and order processing team to work over capacity the last week of most months. It is not like they have extra capacity, they simply run overtime to meet the demand. I have seen overtime beat people into submission. The same story month end after month end wears on people. Add the weekend work and you have a recipe for attrition.

Think about that. The logical action by a salesperson creates an environment that leads people to leave the organization. WHAT ARE WE DOING? Where is the logic in that? On top of the time and a half we are paying at the end of every month, we are compounding the problem by losing trained people who will have to be replaced and their replacements to be trained and that will require more overtime and more employee burnout.

The fallout of the hockey stick does not end there. The after affects are felt in order management as well. The change rate of orders that come in at the end of the period are nearly 300% higher than those that come in during the prior weeks. The order is often touched 4-5 times since the customer usually secured the deal at the lower cost and then makes changes to fit into their supply chain. More non-value-added work. Work that could have been spent elsewhere but is required in the current way of working due to our acceptance of the sales hockey stick.

Next, invoicing gets to feel the stick. Yes, most businesses that flood the supply chain in routine intervals also create an invoicing and collections mess that must be dealt with. High invoicing at the end of the month leads to high accounts receivables that spike at the end of the month. Often, these receivables are out of synch with many automated payment processes and thus the ability of the collections team to reduce them in a timely manner is prohibitive. This leads to an increase in reserves and a constant push on the collections team to "bring in the money". Money that they ultimately cannot bring in due to the automated payment cycles of many customers. The increased demand on these downstream processes is significant and it destroys morale, leads to attrition, and increases waste at nearly every turn. All of this is avoidable.

As if I have not outlined enough of the negative effects of the bonus structure, let me make a short comment on the deal that is "out of the ballpark". You are familiar with these I am sure. These are the deals that no one has heard about, no one has been privy to the possibility and no one has done any preparation for. They show up and BAM! All hell breaks loose. Sure, the saleswoman is getting slapped high five and her bonus is outstanding, but the other 99.5% of the organization is about to feel the negative effects of the deal. Often, these deals are way above the capacity of operations and cannot be delivered as taken. Also, the quantity is often much higher than the raw material suppliers can handle in a short period of time and they are for non-standard products that are much more expensive to produce. A triple negative.

Besides the triple negative, the company needs to spend countless hours harassing their suppliers to get the increased raw material. Many times, they pay premium pricing and expedite fees to get the material. Manufacturing is forced to work overtime in order to raise capacity and let's not forget the inevitable risk of injury that comes from rushing and overexerting and over burdening the work force. The result is rarely positive. The customer is usually affected by a delay in delivery – which does not lead to a positive impression and repeat orders. The procurement team works aggressively to get the raw material in ASAP and often beats up the supplier daily. This makes for a poor relationship with key material suppliers. And manufacturing often has hiccups with quality and safety due to the unnatural demand. There is rarely anything positive generated with these home run orders...... except for the salesperson's personal account.

I am sure you are starting to see the need for lean within the sales processes. And just think, I have only discussed the first issue, the bonus structure.

Next, I want to talk about the misalignment with the Sales, Inventory and Operations Planning (SIOP) process. Yes, there is a process that is intended to bridge the gap and create alignment between sales, operations, and procurement. But, as you might expect, most current state sales processes blow this process up and render it nearly useless.

Most SIOP plans end up being less than 50% accurate. Yes, you can basically flip a coin and get a better result. Many companies try to get better and better at executing the SIOP process. They had meetings and create automated reports and they even go as far as adding resources to do statistical analysis to find the problems. All of these do little to improve the situation. Why? Because they fail to solve one of the main root causes; sales processes that produce widely variable sales volumes in unpredictable patterns. Since the days of Six Sigma, we have known that the ultimate goal of current state operations is to be stable and predictable. If you are not stable and predictable, then you can do no improvement work and you can usually do no planning. Well, at least not any planning that will bare real fruit. Just planning to overcome the obstacles that the unstable and unpredictable sales processes deliver.

Sales processes are like any other process. They take inputs, process them, and produce an output (known as IPO). Every one of them. The inputs and outputs are different, but they each follow the same IPO methodology. With that said, they can be managed to become stable and predictable with application of lean tools and methodologies. Think about the improvement for your company if your SIOP process was around 80% accurate. How much less money would you spend on obsolete inventory? How many less hours of overtime would you run in manufacturing and quoting and order processing? How many less changes would you make to orders on a weekly basis? And how many invoices would fall naturally into the rhythm of the automated payment process that many businesses run today? The answers can be staggering. The savings can also be staggering. And both of those staggering results are attainable if you make the bold decision to drive lean into all sales processes.

The third issue concerning sales is more about morale. Let's be honest, some of the highest paid people in the company are salespeople. Many bonus structures reward them significantly no matter how "hard" or how "easy" the sale is. And they are often paid the same regardless of the downstream inefficiencies that are caused by the processes I mentioned earlier. This does not sit well with the other 90+% of the business that must endure all the waste and headaches that we have discussed. As a matter of fact, they resent it. They see an order that is 40% above their capacity. One that will cause them overtime as well as a few "beat downs" all the while the sales team is off celebrating. Celebrating for securing a sale that was undeliverable as sold and one that they do not have to deal with. That is not teamwork. That is silo goals and silo processes colliding to make a dysfunctional "team".

And the discontent does not stop in manufacturing. Many times, the sales team will extend terms or agree to concessions to secure the deal. They will point to the margin of the sale and how it offsets the extension in the terms or the small concessions that it costs. Sounds great. But it rarely happens that way.

Instead, the process does not pick up on the manual changes so invoices get issued with the standard terms. This leads to disputes, extra processing, and a displeased customer. The concession requires additional contract documentation and special handling and are often missed or not accurately collected during the non-standard process. All this extra processing adds up and all of it eats into the assumed cost of the sale. But, naturally, the salesperson is never docked for these extra costs. The system is not sophisticated enough to account for those charges. So, in the end, the salesperson gets their full bonus, and the rest of the organization must deal with the after mass of the special order. This happens time and time again. And the more it happens, the more dissent is built up against the sales team. Keep in mind, you are not only allowing this to happen. You are encouraging it to happen through your failure to act.

The good news is you can fix this. You can apply the lean principles to your sales processes, and you can create complete alignment across the entire end-to-end value stream. It will not happen overnight, and it will not be easy. But it will pay off dividends in the end because this is probably the number one killer of lean efforts in the business world today. And the number one killer is always the one that produces the biggest payback. So, go after it. Make a difference and your entire team will be better off for it.

3 - Creating KPI's For "Lean"

First, I am a big supporter of key performance indicators (KPI). They are a vital part of most lean operating systems. I am not saying KPIs are bad and that we should not have them. What I am saying is that we should not create KPIs to "justify" the lean work. What does that mean? That means do not create an elaborate dashboard to capture all the savings from "lean" activities. Do not require every site or function to keep records of every kaizen activity to calculate the quantity of activity per team member. Do not create certifications and keep track of the number of Lean Leaders you have running around the company. And, by all means, try your very best not to put a number on any type of maturity assessment you feel compelled to create. Why? Because all of these drive the wrong behaviors. They create non-value-added work, and they will not help you create a culture for lean.

I will talk about how some these well-intended actions lead to the wrong behaviors, but first, I would like to get a little philosophical with you. Lean has been defined in hundreds of different ways. Nearly every consultant has a different spin on it and nearly every big corporation that has "implemented it" has defined it in their own terms. I try not to get caught up in the wisdom of words or the excitement of the burning platform. I look at Lean as the most effective and efficient way to run a business. Just like there are proven formulas for success in sports and other competitive arena, lean has been a proven methodology to win in the game of business.

Here is my point; If you believe that it IS the answer, then why waste time justifying it? Why waste effort and resources capturing data that does little to add value and only fosters a question of commitment? The answer should be to NOT do it. Believe in it and spend all your effort and resources learning how to do it better and better. Ignore the traps suggesting otherwise and prosper from the extra time to focus on learning lean. That will pay dividends down the road and it will not send the wrong signal to the team.

Let me outline a few of the behaviors that your affinity to KPIs drive. First, the calculation of lean savings. This one has two primary issues. On the surface this sounds logical and easy to accept. I mean, why wouldn't we want to keep track of savings so we can tout the awesome benefits from lean. In fact, some would argue that unless we keep track, then we will never know the true benefits of the lean initiative. BINGO! That is exactly why you SHOULD NOT keep track of the savings. OK. I admit I might have lost a few people. Let me elaborate on that last one. By keeping track of the lean savings, you are sending the message that unless we get savings then we might decide not to do this lean thing. You are implying that you need a cost benefit analysis that justifies this lean thing.

Trust me, that is what everyone outside senior leadership sees and reads. And that hurts your employee engagement to learn and it provides the air cover to those who are against it to hold out for failure. It does not matter what you say during your town hall meetings or what you write on your fancy posters and webpage banners. The 98% of the people who are living in the world of process will call your bluff every time.

The second issue associated with calculating the lean savings is the almost immediate conversion of all savings to lean savings. It will take only a few months for the team members to learn that all savings need to be counted as lean savings since there is a target on every manager's performance plan that is tied to the fancy KPI. You will get a swift shift to lean savings and you will mask the progress you are making in some vital areas of the business. Worst yet, you will lose sight to the opportunities you have within the company. In a nutshell, you will make it more difficult to see current state and you will cause many people to manipulate numbers for the sake of a KPI.

Before you say it, I will admit that it would be wrong for any team member to lie about a savings category. You should be able to trust them to have the integrity to not game the system. I passionately believe that. The reality is you will never be able to create a clear enough guideline to manage the way savings are categorized. You will never be able to ensure that any savings that the person used pareto analysis does not get put in the lean bucket. You would be wrong in saying that savings from an action that used a poorly filled out and incomplete A3 should not go into the lean bucket. And you would be silly not to consider the savings derived from a change that was discovered during a Gemba walk not as lean savings. Do you see the difficulty here? Do you see how all this posturing and categorizing is a waste of time and effort and not helping you with your lean culture? I hope so.

Let's move on to the Kaizen per Person KPI. Another easy and common one. This one drives twice the amount of negative behavior than our first one. Why? Because this one will not only be on the manager's performance plan, but it will also likely be added to all employee's performance plans. Now, you have nearly every employee focused on one thing: getting to be part of a kaizen activity. Again, that sounds like a positive thing. I mean who would not want every employee wanting to engage in a kaizen activity. At a high level this is great. But with lean, you should not stop at the *What*. You should move to the *Why* when it comes to behavior.

Ask yourself; Why are people wanting to participate in a kaizen activity? The answer is simple. They need to punch their ticket and get credit. The kaizen is simply a task that they must complete. They are not focused on the learning. They are not engaged on the process of identifying the opportunities for kaizen and they are not even concerned with the improvement that will come from the kaizen. They just want their ticket punched. I have seen this repeatedly. First, you get the group of people who participate in the beginning few months and then are done with lean for the year and then you get the people who wait until the end of the year and the manager always throws together a last-minute kaizen to hit the numbers. In all, the effort is in meeting the target and not in understanding how kaizen is a vital part of the lean system. You will rob them of learning, and you will not be better for it.

The next common action companies take is creating certifications for lean. The aim is to provide a level of knowledge and/or experience the employee attains to earn the certification. Again, the intent is good and logical. If you want to spread the learning and you want to have people strive to excel in their lean journey, then it makes sense to provide them with milestone goals. I wish it would work out that way. Unfortunately, I have not seen one example where this helped support the cultural transformation in a positive way.

The most glaring issue with this is it makes the certification the focus. Not the learning. Right off the bat, you have diverted the attention from your original goal. The certification will naturally be tracked by every manager in the business and there will be end of year goals for each manager. Traditionally these certifications are comprised of a certain amount of training and a certain amount of participation in lean activity (kaizen events, value stream analysis, problem-solving, daily management, etc). What is often lost in the shuffle is the limitation of the resources the company has for each of these criteria.

As an example, I have seen one certification that required a specific training class. The class was only offered once a quarter and had a class size limit of twenty people. Simple math says that the maximum amount of people that can take the class is eighty for the year. If we continue the simple math and apply it to a functional team of 800, it will say that the maximum percent of people in that function that could achieve the certification would be 10%. Well, this one example had a target of 25%. What behavior do you think that drives? Is it all positive behavior? And more importantly, what is the effort being exerted for? That is right, the training. They just want to check the box of training. I will cover the checklist lean issues in a later chapter, but I think you can clearly see the problem with this metric.

The aim was good but what it has led to is a focus on a class and frustration with an impossible goal. Many will realize that they cannot get the class and will drop all efforts in getting the certification. You have just made the certification a painful topic and you have just turned many people against lean in general because they will associate it with yet another unachievable goal.

The other negative consequence of the certification KPI is the ensuing spiking of the ball once it is complete. People will naturally assume that they have mastered lean and are done learning. Yes, many of the companies that have certifications have a series of them. No matter which one the person achieves they will still feel like they are at the maximum amount of learning they need for that level and they will not look to deepening their understanding of the lean principles. This will hinder your company's progress as well as the potency of the application of the lean tools. In short, you will not get the in-depth understanding of lean and you will only get superficial benefits.

The last KPI I will discuss is the maturity score. Yes, everyone seems to love, love, love a fancy maturity model. I have seen some impressive models in my time and each and every one of them have been introduced with great intentions and each and every one of them created the same poor behaviors. It doesn't matter if it is a colorful spider diagram or a twenty-four criteria matrix with four distinct levels of achievement, they all lead to the same issues.

Issue one is the most obvious, a goal. You can try to keep numbers off the model. I tried four times. But it does not seem to matter. The masses will demand either numbers or letters or some form of grading system. The very second you put it on the model, you will provide the goal to the team. We must remember; we are talking about transforming culture. Hard stuff. When you have a culture that has been used to setting goals and creating checklists for nearly everything, then you will naturally be fighting against the tendency to incorporate that into the "new normal". Do not let it happen. It will be like giving a person who is trying to stop drinking soda a diet coke. It is still a soda and it is reinforcing the old way of working. Do not let it happen. I know this one sounds petty, but it is a big issue. Let me continue with this thought.

Let's say we developed a model and it have five areas of performance. And each area has 3 levels of maturity. So, you can either score a 1, 2 or 3 in five different area of performance. How clear do you think you can make the differences between a 1 and a 2? Or a 2 and a 3? Can you be so clear that every single manager would grade the very same way regardless of who they are measuring? In other words, how good is your Gauge R&R (I had to throw that in for my Six Sigma friends)? My experience says that it is poor at best. Every manager is at a different level of their own understanding of lean therefore they will certainly see things differently. The result is inconsistent grading across the organization. An average grade of 2.3 in one function could have better true lean maturity than a score of 3.1 in a different organization. I hear you. I know. We should have the lean leaders do the assessment with the manager. That makes sense. So, will you have a lean leader for each function? Will you have the same lean manager complete the assessment each and every time? Are you going to have one dedicated lean leader run all over the company and do every single assessment to ensure consistency? Of course not.

The intent of any maturity model is to provide an assessment to the team on how well they are progressing in their journey. It provides them areas where to focus and it provides them a gauge to compare one month to the previous month and one quarter to the previous quarter. If you utilize it for that purpose, then it will be worth its weight in gold. To do that, I strongly suggest you do not use numbers and, if you do, do not set goals for each team to hit a certain number by a certain date. The consistency is enough of any issue to steer away from doing this. The other is the same thing I pointed out earlier; you will shift the focus from the learning to the number. The team will focus on only the number and fail to dedicate their efforts on the deep learning and reflection that can help them advance so much faster through the curve.

The last point I will make is the creation of non-value-added work involved with these measures. All too often, these measures are tracked manually. Even the best teams, end up spending time each week updating scorecards and inputting data into shared files. Even the best governance for shared documents results in countless opportunities for mistakes. This is especially frustrating when the data is pure non-value-added information.

Then there is the person who must consolidate all the data and produce multiple reports for senior leadership. This all takes time, and it is all for nothing more than reporting. I have seen these requirements grow from a part of one persons' responsibility to consuming nearly two full time resources in a matter of six months.

The lure is that there are always different ways to look at the data and there are always different buckets of savings coming into scope. This adds up quickly and it is compounded across the organization. The "central team" that is consolidating and providing all the reporting usually requires more and more input from the various business teams. So, in addition to the resources fully dedicated to the reporting, you have multiple people spending 5-10% of their time supporting reporting requirements. This is pure waste. And on top of that, it is usually the "lean team" that is causing and executing this wasteful activity. What kind of example is that for the organization?

Think about this. If lean is the right decision, why do you have to create an entire team and reporting structure to prove it? Measuring it as if it needs to be justified will send a message to the organization that someday the payback will reduce to a point of you moving on to the next shiny object. That could take a year or three years, no one will know. But one thing for sure, there will be a portion of the team who is disengaged and is waiting for that day to come. Hiding in the background, doing nothing to change because they have seen the flavor of the month far too many times. Do not feed their appetite. Make the decision and then spend all that time and effort in learning lean; not measuring it.

4 - Giving Senior Leaders Too Much Time To Get It

Lean leadership is different from traditional leadership. I often say it is 180 degrees different. Anything in the traditional leadership world can be referenced as the 180-degree opposite in the lean leadership world. You have heard many of these differences. To be specific, here are a few of the most common:

Traditional Leader	Lean Leaders
Direct action and activity	Coach team to develop actions/activity
Develop solutions for problems	Help the team solve their problems themselves
Have meetings to review performance	Go to the place where the work happens to see performance
Make all/most of the decisions for the team	Facilitate the decision-making process for the team
Ask questions to find failure or gaps	Ask questions to learn
Hide or distract attention from problems	Develop processes that highlight problems
Focus on holding PEOPLE accountable	Focus on holding the PROCESS accountable
Drive the execution of the plan	Enable the team to execute the plan
Present and speak for the team	Allow the team to speak for themselves
Assume to GET respect	Always GIVE respect

Like I said, these are just a few of the common differences. The point I want to make is that being a leader in the lean world is totally different than being a leader in the traditional business world. George Koensaeker said it best in his book **"Leading the Lean Enterprise Transformation"**. He wrote "Lean is Leadership Intensive". I do not know if this is the exact message George was going for, but, for me this means that Leaders have the most intensive amount of change to make in the lean world. They are the ones who must change the who, what, where, when and why they do nearly everything! This is a big deal, and this is a critical deal. Why? Because no matter how long you try, no matter how many training sessions you provide and no matter how many times you say it in email, town halls or other media platforms, people will ALWAYS, ALWAYS, ALWAYS follow their leaders. It is a fact of human nature that we all need to accept and move on from. Move on from but do something about.

   Lean is about respect for people. All people. That includes leaders. With that said, we should give people in leadership the same respect that we give everyone else in the organization. With that respect comes the expectation that they need to learn what lean is just like everyone else. Think about it. Let's say you have a woman who has learned how to progress up the ranks of the traditional corporate ladder and she is a Vice President of Operations. The leadership team then decides to embark on a lean journey. Should we expect her to instantly know how to be a lean leader? Of course not. That would be disrespectful to her. Just like we should not expect her to understand, we should not expect the front-line managers to understand and we should not expect the middle managers to understand... on day one.

You need to provide them the opportunity to learn the new way of leading.

This learning should include several aspects. The best examples of this are companies that do some time of immersion. This is hands on training for the leaders to actually learn the fundamentals of lean firsthand and on the job. These are not PowerPoint sessions or fancy conferences. These are roll up your sleeves, get a little sweaty and do the work yourself type of training. I highly encourage you to do this for your leadership team. It shows them your dedication to them learning and it reinforces the importance of leading in a different way.

Once you have provided the training and the reinforcement, it is the leaders responsibility to start to change. This process should be supported by coaching and routine reflection with a lean leader within the company or from a lean consultant. These people are your face of the company and the people who your team members look to for queues on how to act, so you need to put ample time and resource into aiding their conversion. I also highly recommend the leadership team spend a good amount of time together as a group to reflect on the overall progress as well as their individual progress. This will help provide opportunities for them to coach each other and it will make it more common for them to admit shortcomings to each other. The strongest teams are ones who speak openly about their shortcomings and find ways for others to help bridge the gap for the sake of the team. With that said, this is not a free pass for someone to decide not to change. On the contrary. This is where they need to hold each other accountable to change.

This takes time. Again, out of respect, they should be afforded time. Time …… but not eternity. Yes, this is where respect can quickly be replaced by complacency. I do not have a specific timeline on when a person should be able to change. Some change quickly and some take a few more cycles to catch on. Either way, you need to pay awfully close attention to the leader's actions and make very sure that any non-lean action is addressed immediately. I say immediately not to inflict punishment, but to reinforce the lean way. When people are learning something new, it does not come natural and they can often fall back into their old ways. If they are not alerted to this, then they will never make the lean behavior a new habit. They will get stuck and that will not be good for the organization. You owe it to them to help them make the change.

I have spent a decent amount of time outlining how you need to support the leaders in your organization with the transformation to lean leadership. Now, I would like to point out some specific issues that arise when the transformation takes too long.

First, it is natural to have around 20% of the team not wanting to change. Does not matter how small or how large the team is, 20% seems to be the number. This segment of the team can be loud, or they can be quiet, but rest assured, they are not ready and eager to change. So, when they see a sign, and I mean any sign of hope that change will not be required, they will cling to it like a life vest. Trust me, they are looking for those signs on a daily basis.

Remember when I said that people will always follow their leaders. Well, this is a perfect example of why it is a big issue when leaders do not change. All it takes for some is to see the routine PowerPoint meetings in the conference room continuing to be a sign of relief. A simple cancellation of a Gemba walk is reinforcement that "this lean thing might not happen". If they can survive a few more months, then some will think this whole mess will go away for good.

This is feeding the defiance. This is fueling the nay-sayers, and this is what starts to rub the initial followers the wrong way. No one wants to make a personal effort to change and then see their leader not changing and, worst yet their peers holding them back and not having any consequences for doing it. The team dynamic is vital to the success of the overall business. If you allow this to fester and to continue, then you will have a larger problem to deal with down the road. It will not go away on its own.

A second issue that presents itself when leaders fail to change is inconsistent company culture. As I mentioned in a previous chapter, all efforts should be focused on being stable and predictable. This goes for company culture as well. It should not matter if you work in finance or operations, the culture should be the same. People in procurement should not have a different expectation when it comes to lean that those in human resources or engineering. Consistency matters. Your customers purchase your entire value stream. They do not buy your engineering function alone and they do not only purchase your IT team. The value stream provides the products and/or services and they need to flow across all of them as effectively and efficiently as they can to maximize customer satisfaction and margin. You cannot get this if the IT leader is pretending to support lean. The more they pretend, the more people will observe it and the more they will decide that lean is just going to happen in IT.

That is enough of a reason to act. But that is not where it ends. Because we are an end-to-end value stream, all the functions interact in some way. So, when that person in operations reaches out to the team in procurement for help with a problem-solving activity and that procurement team has put lean on the shelf until the beginning of the next quarter, then you will quickly begin to erode your momentum. Teams talk. Processes talk. And when they are talking different languages then the unfortunate conclusion is usually, they all migrate back to the original normal. This might take six months, or it might take a year. Either way, it will happen.

Just think about all that progress going down the drain, all because you allowed one function to not engage. Just one. There is an old saying in the Navy; *"On the strength of one link in the cable, Dependeth the might of the chain. Who knows when thou mayest be tested? So, live that thou bearest the strain!"* This is exactly what must be done with leadership. You never know which leader will be tested, so you must ensure they are ALL ready and willing to support the strain. Lean transformation is not a piece of cake. It is not simple. It requires learning many different ways of working. Allowing one leader to return the whole company to square one is a devastating mistake. Search them out and eventually sift them out if they are not willing to make the change.

My last point is a little off topic. Meaning, it is more of a recommendation than pointing out a problem with behavior. I spoke about the challenge involved with leader making the transformation. It can be hard for some and to be frank, some will not want to change. Some like the traditional way of leading. Lean leadership does not appeal to them. I suggest that you spend a good amount of time upfront discussing this with every leader. If a leader is not a supporter then make every effort to help them with a very soft landing. Hard landings send the wrong signal. Make it soft for the volunteers. It will pay off in dividends down the road.

This will naturally open at least one role. Fill that role with someone who already knows and lives lean leadership. I assume you will hire a Lean Leader to help to get the lean journey started. That role will need help with the heavy lifting on the front end. Having this "extra" lean leader onboard will help immensely with the progress. In the uncommon event that every member of the team is eager to become lean leaders, then you might want to think about adding a role to the leadership team. Call it a Chief of Staff or a Change Management leader or another title. Regardless of what you call it, make sure you hire a proven lean leader in the role. Many hands make for light lifting. True for lifting and true for cultural change.

5 - Turning Lean Into A Checklist

I mentioned this topic in a previous chapter. I have found this to be one of the most frustrating issues to deal with. Partly because many of these checklists are introduced by LEAN LEADERS! Yes, the people who are there to help facilitate and foster the journey towards lean leadership and a lean culture are the same ones who often introduce this problem into the picture. The other reason is that I believe that process checklists can also be hugely beneficial tools. Yes, I am on both sides of this coin so allow me to try to give you both perspectives.

I want to revisit a point I made earlier. Lean transformation is different, and it can be confusing at times. With that said, it makes it harder to transition to a new way of working (lean) when you are using tactics or strategies from the old way of working. It perpetrates a return to the old way, and it makes people believe they can just incorporate some of the "lean stuff" into their own way of working and they will be good to go. That is wrong and that is unfair in my opinion. You are basically making it even harder for them to change when you try to help them bring some of the legacy tools with them. Keep this in mind as I discuss this checklist mentality and tools.

I believe in coaching aides. I believe there are a lot of things to learn and no one can learn them all at one time. Coaching aides and quick access cards can be good. I also think they can be bad. Take a common topic like problem solving. Most companies have some type of formal problem-solving structure (A3's, 8-Step, PDCA and some even create confusing acronyms that spell out things that are often confused with other acronyms – try not to do that). The structure is taught in a training environment and then the real learning is supposed to come with the application of the process.

This usually involves people who have not been to the training and it is often forced into action based on a requirement from the training class. Yes, I have seen several companies who have rendered the satisfactory completion of the training class to be a completed problem-solving activity by the training participant. One of the tools that the trainees are given are coaching cards. These cards vary in depth of content, but they commonly have questions to ask and criteria to meet during each phase of the problem-solving process. The card is supposed to help them become better problem solvers since it walks them thru a list of things to do. In other words, it gives them a checklist to fill out to become a better problem solver.

This sounds fantastic. It sounds like an effective tool. In reality, it causes confusion, and it hurts more than it helps. Confusion enters when the team is not able to answer every question. This is natural since you cannot think of every possible scenario and therefore you cannot develop the perfect list of questions. There are bound to be several questions that just will not apply to every problem. So, which questions are good and which ones are bad? Can I proceed with only answering one of the five questions or are we required to answer at least two? You get the point. Confusion soon turns into frustration since each and every phase brings more and more questions. Soon the team becomes so frustrated that they deem the process to be a waste of time, too much work and not helpful. This usually sends them back to their old way of solving problems and taking one giant step backwards in your lean journey.

Problem solving is just one area that this checklist tool hurts. A second place is leader standard work (LSW). Leader standard work is as important to a robust lean operating system as process standard work. Most people who understand LSW agree with that statement. This is yet another topic that is taught and then intended to be applied. The application can be easy …… if lean leaders would just let it be easy. Instead, we cling to standards as a pillar and demand that people follow a specific template. We cite consistency and a common language as support for the forced template. In the end, the template becomes so complex and tedious to fill out that it is often only partly filled in and most people consider it a one and done event. They fill it out and say they have LSW and thus they have checked off that box. They are officially a leader who embraces LSW.

The problem is next to no one can explain the purpose of the LSW. On top of that, none of them can find their sheet a week later and those that did manage to save it did not fill in any of the comment fields and thus it is just a piece of paper. We have turned the tool and component of the lean operating system into a piece of paper that must be filled out in a certain way and with specific information. We have robbed the team of learning how LSW fits into the operating system and have replaced their personal creativity in incorporating it into their daily routine with an 8X10 piece of paper. All in the name of standardization and with helpful intentions.

I have heard over a hundred people say they would use LSW if they could just be left to record it the way they want. If they are forced to complete the standard template, they will go through the motions and not think more about it. Is that the reaction we want? I know it's not. So, let's make sure we make the learning about the tool and allow the team members to decide how to incorporate the tool into their personal routine in order to get the most benefit for the business. It is a vital part of the lean operating system so we can't afford to have it be wasted.

The next area I want to highlight is the blanket directives. One of the most common ones is having a team performance board. These have several different names; huddle boards, QDIP boards, Daily Management boards, and the list goes on and on). The purpose of the board is easy; to measure the effectiveness of the process performance in a nutshell. I could go on for over three pages discussing the true purpose of daily management, but I want to focus on the broad directive. Shortly after the broad directive, there is usually a slew of training conducted and the teams are then expected to put up their boards and start doing daily management. Sounds easy enough. But, just like all the other easy things, this is a recipe for disaster.

My experience shown that people cannot learn the purpose and execution of daily management in a PowerPoint training class. Assuming they can is simply a poor assumption and one that will lead to more bad than good. What typically happens is within a certain period of time, there will be a bunch of wonderfully decorated "production boards" on the walls of the office or the shop floor. The team will stand in front of it according to the suggestion of the trainer and they will be "doing lean daily management". Box checked. Success and completion. Sadly, this reminds me of one of my favorite movies; *What About Bob*". In the movie, the main character, Bob, is literally tied to the mast of a sailboat and he and a few friends are out on the water. With great excitement and a huge sense of accomplishment, Bob screams "I'm Sailing". No Bob, you are not sailing. You are tied to a mast of a sailboat and the other people are the one's doing the sailing. Just like Bob, these team members are not doing lean daily management. And yet, your actions have led them to believe they are.

False beliefs are dangerous in lean transformations. They are dangerous because they lead to an expectation and they often lead to an evaluation of the aspect surrounding the false belief. In the daily management example, the scenario usually plays out like this. First, the team checks the box and makes the board. Then they stand in front of the board and the manager usually reads the charts and everyone stands there until she is done. This repeats itself for several weeks or months. Then, after that, the team begins to question why they must do this meeting that takes too long and has not done anything for them. The manager can only agree and wonder the same question. With little support they usually decide to stop meeting as often and put the board on the back burner. The board stays there until the senior leader announces that they are visiting. Then the team spends hours updating the board and making sure all the charts are nice and colorful for the big visit. This is the positive scenario.

The negative scenario is where you do your same routine and have your meetings in the conference rooms during your visit and the team does not have to bring the board out of hibernation. Either way, the team has decided that "daily management" doesn't work, and the board is a waste of time. Any attempt to change their mind will take triple the effort and it still might not work. You have set them up for failure by making the daily management board a checklist action and it will be one more nail in your lean efforts coffin.

Daily management boards are just one of the common directives. Others are the # of Kaizen events, the roll out of an audit process and a published list of improvement opportunities. Each of these are good things if done right. Meaning, if they are part of the natural maturity of the team or organization then they are beneficial. Artificially injecting them into the maturity curve does nothing more than create a box to check and that is usually all you get from it.

Lean is a journey. Every journey is different, and every journey needs to progress in its own way. The main driver of the journey should be problems. You should constantly be solving the next biggest problem in the organization. Each function and each team within the function should be solving their own biggest problems. No two teams will have the same exact problems and therefore no two team should incorporate daily management boards at the same exact time. They should also not be required to do the same quantity of kaizen events per year or to begin doing process audits simply because the senior leader decides it needs to happen everywhere. Put your effort into coaching each team to run their own race, to solve their own problems. This will serve you much better and it will help facilitate the key learning of how these tools and processes fit into the lean operating system. That learning will catapult your lean efforts at a much faster velocity than any of your standard directives could ever do.

Before I leave this chapter, I want to provide the perspective in favor of checklists. As with everything in lean, the WHY is always important. I believe the checklist is a beneficial tool if the WHY is to facilitate the effective and efficient execution of the process with a first-time-right result. Add to that, the safety of all involved in the process. A few examples. In the beginning it was near impossible to find a pilot who could fly the B17 Bomber safely. There were countless issues and significant accidents and deaths associated with the aircraft. Finally, they developed a checklist for the pilot to use. The benefit was almost instant. You see, the B17 was a very complex system and in order to follow a complex process safely and effectively, there needed to be a checklist tool to aid the pilot. This is a perfect case for a checklist. It is enhancing the PROCESS. It is not taking the place of the pilot's behavior which is what my examples above were pointing out.

A second example of a good use of a checklist is in the operating room. Several hospitals have implemented surgery checklist for the team to align on BEFORE the tray of scalpels and other surgical tools are even permitted in the operating room. A simple alignment on patient name, surgery type, left or right side, blood type and a few other safety measures are now part of the process of ensuring a safe and effective surgery. Again, the checklist is part of the PROCESS. It is not taking place of the persons behavior.

6 - Misunderstanding the Basic Concepts of Lean

I want to start this chapter with a short training session. I mentioned that countless consultants have defined lean in hundreds of different ways. And nearly every company who has implemented lean has done it in their own way. Many tried to model the Toyota Production System (TPS) because they seem to be the most notable company doing lean. And many have developed their own Operating System that begins with their company name. What is the same amongst all of these differences is the principles of lean and the main disrupters of lean.

The five principles of lean are commonly stated as:

1) Deliver Value in the Eyes of the Customer
2) Drive optimization across the Value Stream
3) Create Flow in your Value Stream
4) Aim to achieve Pull in your Value Stream
5) Always seek perfection

There is universal agreement on these. The other universal agreement is the disrupters of Lean. They are:

1) Waste
2) Unevenness
3) Overburden

Yes, I used the English words. There are some Japanese words that many like to use but I usually mess up a vowel or two when I say them, so I stick to what I know. Now that we have aligned on these universal truths, let's look at the common misunderstanding and subsequent behaviors that I have observed in nearly every place I have worked. These misunderstandings cause a significant amount of problems for the team and they are huge motivation killers for the organization.

My first one is a tricky topic, Perfection. Seeking perfection is one of the five principles of lean. I believe in the pursuit of perfection. The tricky part is how do you seek it? And is it attainable? The common thought is that you foster a problem solving and continuous improvement culture and that will allow you to seek perfection. The more problems you solve and the more improvement activity that you do the better the process is and the better the results. I agree with all of this.

Where the issue arises is when you expect continuous improvement on EVERYTHING. I know, I know. Toyota does 1,200 kaizen per day. Or something crazy like that. Side note – do you ever wonder how anyone came up with that number? And isn't is sort of a waste of time counting them? I mean, what does it prove? Are they going to stop doing lean if they fall to 900 because the payback is dropping off and thus not worth the effort and investment? Sorry, I digress. Back to my point, expecting continuous improvement on everything is a certain lean effort killer. First, it is impossible. There is no way that you will hire enough people to actively work on improving every single process in the company. No way. So, why make the action an expectation?

I will admit that there is a little bit of a difference for this topic when we look at manufacturing and non-manufacturing processes. For manufacturing processes, one could argue that the team that is doing proper daily management and the related problem-solving processes are indeed doing continuous improvement on everything. One can say that the end-to-end value stream is being improved continuously. I will give you that at a high level. But when you go to the very next level that falls apart.

Most manufacturing processes have at least five steps to them. I am being very general in that statement, but it's pretty close. I guarantee you that you are not looking at improving every single step in the process at the same time. You are simply solving the step with the biggest problem and then moving to the next problem and the next repeatedly. Therefore, you are not continuously improving everything all the time. But I will say that manufacturing processes have a much higher opportunity to be worked on routinely. Non-manufacturing processes are a completely different story.

I worked in manufacturing for nearly fifteen years. I know it is hard work. So, don't close this book with my next few sentences. The reason non-manufacturing processes are different is that there is a bigger challenge in driving improvement in these processes. The challenge is not in the processes themselves. They are no more complex or difficult than manufacturing processes. The challenge is in the way we manage the processes.

Unfortunately, we do not actually manage the processes. We manage the resources doing the processes. What that means, is we raise the utilization of the resource by requiring them to perform multiple processes all at the same time. Yes, at the same time. To compare this to a manufacturing scenario, it would be like having a station that places a few screws in the back of a refrigerator and then the next time they connect a wire to a light curtain module and the next cycle they drill shut the casing on a solenoid valve and the next cycle they are required to finish the final edge on a ceramic pot. Do you get the point? This is exactly what we require a non-manufacturing person to do on a daily basis.

It is obvious that we are driving unevenness in the above scenario. That is just one bad thing about it. What I typically see is a compounded negative affect by assuming the team will drive improvement activity in all their processes. This is just not possible. What we must realize, is there are some processes that are just good enough as is. I know that sounds like cursing coming from a lean guy, but that is the truth. We (you) simply will not hire enough people to manage improvement activity on every single process these team members are required to do. Take Accounts Receivables. A team member routinely performs the following processes at a minimum:

1) Reconcile account statements
2) Register disputes
3) Apply credits to accounts
4) Apply payments to accounts
5) Print and/or email invoices

You can see they perform multiple processes and they bounce around back and forth all day long. The team probably performs many of these processes at a level that meets the current customers' expectation. My point is that we should not try to exceed the expectation in the name of continuous improvement. This would be over-processing, which is one of the lean wastes. The improvement activity should be focused on the process not meeting expectation or the one with the biggest problem keeping the team from being efficient. So, yes, sometimes current state will not be perfect, but it will be good enough.

Another misunderstanding is closely related to continuous improvement; Problem solving (PS). So many senior leaders fail to understand the problem-solving process. The amount of stress and overburden this misunderstanding causes can be staggering and it is also the cause of a great deal of negative feelings towards lean. This is critical because problem solving is one of the three core foundations for lean process management: Standard work, Daily Management and Problem Solving/Kaizen.

As I stated, most companies have some form of structured problem solving within their lean operating system. At least they aim to. One would think that we would require the senior leaders to learn and fully understand the PS process BEFORE they are unleashed on the organization to "coach and mentor" folks on it. Sadly, this is not the case. I have seen some of the worst behaviors by senior leaders in PS than any other process. Second only to lean coaching. I will cover lean coaching in the next chapter, for now let's dig deeper into PS.

First, problem solving is a process. Not an instantaneous action or one day event. This means it takes time and there are natural milestones associated with good robust problem solving. I have used four different models over my career. Each one had milestones and each one had guidelines and expectations for said milestones. The training was always clear when it came to the requirement and time allowances for these milestones. With all that background, it is frustrating to observe so many senior leaders fail to follow the guidelines and allow the problem-solving team to follow the process. The most common behavior I observe is the reluctance to provide a reasonable amount of time to perform the work.

What does this time crunch do and why does it hurt your lean efforts? It might sound contradictory, but one thing it does is PROLONG the PS process. Yes, it makes the process take longer than it should. There are many reasons why it takes longer. One, the team will usually cling to the first "great" idea when it arises. This is especially common when they are lacking timely data to use. Taking the first idea and running with it will lead the team down a path that they will rarely ever back away from. Therefore, they will continue the rest of the process with the selected "root cause" and will often meet your deadline with a mediocre solution. The mediocre solution will be met with an outward display of disappointment and the need to return to the PS process to "get it right this time".

Do you see the triple negative reaction the senior leader caused? One, the team failed to follow the process to narrow down to a few possible root causes. Instead, they went with the first one. Two, the team is dejected with the mediocre outcome and likely very disengaged in the thought of continuing the process. An, three, the leader blames the team for the poor performance. I did not even mention the rework that is now required and the waiting time for the best-known solution to ultimately be implemented.

  I wish I could say this is a far-fetched scenario, but I can't. I have witnessed it repeatedly. It is terribly sad to see the effect on the morale of the team and it is frustrating to hear the reasoning and justification that many senior leaders use for this behavior; We must act with urgency. We must make this a top priority and lean in with more effort. Our customers do not care how long it takes us or how many hours we need to work to find a solution – they just want a solution. All of these are a bunch of senior leaders BS. Excuse my French, but that is all it is to everyone else in the organization besides the senior leaders who are destroying the PS process due to THEIR OWN lack of experience with the process. Stop this from happening. Coach your senior leaders on the process and have them prove to be effective coaches BEFORE you allow them to be involved with the process. The rest of the team will make significant improvement without their interference. Trust me.

  The second area around PS that senior leader's stifle progress is the data analysis. Let me state upfront that data is a requirement of PS. If you have no data, then THAT is the first problem you need to solve. Yes, the fishbone diagram is a great tool for theorizing or creating a list of possible root causes, but I still contend that you should still go get real data on the selected "root cause" before you officially start your problem-solving process. This implies that the process might not get to start for a reasonable period of time to collect data. This is often a bone of contention with senior leaders. They want immediate action and do not see data collection as an appropriate action. Fact is, it is a required action in the absence of data and therefore, you need to provide that time. Keep in mind, I will almost bet one hundred bucks that data collection is part of your structured problem-solving process, so let the team follow your process.

Next, the actual analysis itself. Many times, the data analysis will not show a clear winner when it comes to stratification. Nothing will stand way out. This can be frustrating and prolong the decision-making process since there is no clear path that is screaming, "pick me" to the team. Those that are familiar with pareto analysis and sample size determination are experienced in selecting the first level of root causes to dig deeper into. They understand that the first pass through the cycle will often address a lower percentage of the overall problem then the team had hoped. There is never a silver bullet and there is rarely a level one issue that accounts for more than 30-40% of the problem.

The danger comes when an inexperienced leader decides that the team needs to do things like combine buckets of data at the level one to address "80% of the problem". This is quite common, and it is the result of the misunderstanding of the 80/20 Rule. In general, the 80/20 Rule states that 80% of your problem will be tied to 20% of your inputs. It does not mean that you must tackle 80% of your problem in your PS process and it does not mean you have to take a sample size of 80% for your data analysis. I think it is obvious, how these two misunderstandings can cause a significant amount of over-processing and wasted activity and confusion within the team. Not to mention, it almost always forces the team to combine buckets to meet the 80% directive. This is like adding a bucket of oranges to a bucket of pears and then doing data analysis to figure out the common problem. Foolish and simply wrong. Learn the 80/20 Rule first before you engage with the team to coach them in their data analysis. It will save the whole team a great deal of time and will also allow for a proper analysis of the data to be conducted.

The last topic I will discuss is Standardization. This is yet another area where us Lean Leaders steer the team down the wrong path. Or at least down the narrow and bumpy path. As a reminder, I will state that we are all in agreement that we are trying to incorporate stable and predictable process performance in our operations. Stable and predictable process performance is a requirement for process improvement to start. The typical first step to achieve stable and predictable is the creation, agreement, and implementation of Standard work. Or standard work instructions or whatever your company calls them. Bottom line, we start with having standards for our process work.

Now that we agree on that, I will quote a wise leader I had the privilege to work with, Todd Wymann. Todd made the enlightened statement that "standardization does not mean one standard". This is a brilliant statement and one that underscores the massive misunderstanding of the concept of standardization. I will outline three examples of how this misunderstanding hinders your progress and completely disengages your team members.

One, selecting a rigid set of performance measures for the company and requiring every function to implement them. Not just implement them; but also have them on every team member performance plans. I will admit, it seems like a good idea to have standard goals. Especially for manufacturing. I mean all manufacturing is the same .... Right? Quality is paramount to customer satisfaction so First Time Right should be an obvious performance measure to have for every site. And why wouldn't we measure Units per Employee at every site and have a common goal of a 25% improvement. Just makes sense – doesn't it? I think you are catching on a little.

The reality is that even common manufacturing sites are different. I worked in a refrigeration plant early in my career. We made top mount no frost refrigerators. A sister plant also made refrigerators. The only difference was they made side-by-sides. Still another sister plant made large top mount units. Standardization would say we should all have the same quality measure. First time Right should be tracked at all three sites and we should each have the same goals. Reality proves this to be a poor decision. Why? Because it would have forced all three plants to focus on the same measure and ASSUME that the measure is the biggest problem for the site. In reality, that was not true. We had significantly different problems to deal with and we had significantly different processes in many of the most complex process areas.

One size does not fit all. Assuming it does and requiring it to fit will lead to a misalignment to the critical focus for the site and will often create a situation where one site will meet the target with no effort and another site will struggle to come within the same quartile of the goal. Both are a waste, and both are not how you should approach performance measure selection and target setting. I will discuss this in more detail in the next chapter.

A second mistake leaders make with standardization is dictating standard templates... for everything from production boards to meeting notes. Standards for the sake of standards in the name of Standardization. I agree there should be standards, but I believe they should be standard at the process level. Forcing standardization at the adoption/execution level not only stifles creativity, it robs the team of the learning and it shows disrespect to them in general.

As an example, I once tried to implement production boards in a manufacturing site. I worked with a brilliant black belt on my team and we came up with the master template. Then we put up the boards in all the main production areas. Then we told the team to start using them.

At the time, I thought this was fair. Three weeks later we had a team meeting and used the time to walk around and look at all the boards. Much to my surprise, they were the same as when we put them up three weeks later. Not a single weekly chart was updated, and they schedule on the board was still the production schedule from the week we erected the boards. When I voiced my displeasure, the team responded with a very humbling message; They were not part of the creation of the board and therefore did not understand the board and therefore did not feel compelled to change anything about the board. Basically, they were my boards so they assumed I would update them. Wow. What a lesson. A good lesson. An accurate lesson. I had failed to teach them anything and I had failed to engage them in the development of the board and therefore, I showed a great deal of disrespect in requiring them to just use them.

After that wake-up call, we took a reasonable amount of time to explain the purpose of the boards as well as the way they fit in the weekly review process. Almost immediately, each team had revised their boards to meet THEIR NEED'S and we began the journey to learning how to maximize the effectiveness of the tool moving forward. And, yes, every board was different, but every team had a board, and every team used the board as part of the weekly review process and as the focus point for problem solving. Do not steal the learning from the team. Give them the Why and let them develop the How and the What. They own the process, so they should own the way to adhere to the process.

7 - The Rest of the Top Ten

The first five are indeed the most ignored and the most impactful in my opinion. They are the ones that Employee Engagement surveys will fail to identify, and they are the ones that most people will just not tell you. Some of the reason is they do not think you will do anything about it. And some of it is they do not actually see their own disengagement as a problem. Especially, those that are fine with "lean failing". They find comfort in the issues and they hope they continue. We can discuss how to deal with this segment of the team later in this chapter, but I want to first discuss some of the more visible actions that senior leaders do that are total lean killers. These are not in any special order.

#6 – Constantly changing in the name of continuous improvement

This can be very frustrating and demoralizing to the team. The obvious reason is that is never allows the team to be stable and predictable. It puts them in a constant churn, and it will wear them out after a few cycles. Remember what I said earlier, we cannot hire enough resources to attempt to make everything perfect. Stable and predictable is the first goal. For many processes, this should be the final goal. Constantly bumping it up to just drive a continuous improvement culture is creating a culture where we waste valuable resources focusing on low value work. That is not efficient. Many times, the original goal is tied to a customer expectation. Exceeding an expectation is fine for some performance measures. For others, exceeding is simply over-processing. In other word, waste.

A second example of constantly changing is for long-term goals. Many times, you will develop a plan of action to get to the goal. The team will then begin to complete the activity to make steps towards the goal. What I have witnessed too often is the senior leader jumping in after a short period and questioning why they are not at the goal yet. As if it was possible to reach the goal in the short period and while ignoring the fact that she had signed off on the long-term plan of action. The disrespect for the process is one thing, but what makes it worse is when that same leader criticizes the team's performance and starts to question every single aspect of the original plan. This compounds the frustration, and it deflates the energy to drive forward.

On top of those issues, what makes it a triple negative is when the leader forces the team to re-do their plan. This not only reduces their confidence in their ability to execute it also prolongs negates much of the prior work and renders it useless and a waste. There is a reason long term plans are called long term. Don't rush to judgement after one month and create rework and frustration just because you feel compelled to push the team harder. You will do far more harm than good, and you will destroy any positive momentum in your lean effort.

The last example I will highlight in this area is constantly changing the focus of the effort. Some call this scope creep. This is where you are driving the team to drive improvement in a specific area of the business and then you decide to change it a short time later.

An example: I worked for one company where we began to focus on invoice disputes for a specific product line. The team did the proper value stream analysis and created an action plan to reduce the dispute dollars to an agreed to goal. Work was going well, and they were making good progress. Then, leadership decided that we could not afford to just focus on one product line, so they brought in the other two product lines into the scope. Naturally, this required mapping of the other two processed and additional actions for the plan. We did not add resources to over the additional work. Just more work.

About a month later the team started falling behind on execution. They simply could not handle the increased amount of activity. At this point, you would think that leadership would ask some questions and see if the team needed help. Instead, leadership decided that we could not afford to only focus on equipment sales, we needed to include the service business in the effort. We had to fix it all not just one small area. I will not bore you with the details of how this constant changing scope led to a disengaged team that had significant turnover (voluntary) and that never reached the first milestone goal. I think it is obvious and I hope you see that lean is not about doing it all AT THE SAME TIME. It is about solving your biggest problem first and then using those learning to make improvements in other areas that it applies. A scope is a scope for a reason. If you do not keep the scope the same, you will only make it less likely for any progress to be made. And you will kill some of your enthusiasm for your lean effort.

#7 Irrational expectations

Back in the early 2000's there was this cool fad in the improvement space called BHAGS. It stands for Big Hairy Audacious Goals. The thought process was to create these crazy goals in an effort to get people to think so far out of the whelm of possibility that you might find some breakthrough ideas to deliver super awesome benefits. I participated in one session and I thought the process was fine, but it really didn't do much to create innovative thinking. I am sure others have had better success, but I just did not see the value in the exercise. This leads me to a similar topic, irrational goals and expectations.

Lean is fundamentally about respect. The best lean leaders are very respectful, and they let respect for people guide them in their coaching. Irrational goals and expectations are the opposite of respect. When I say irrational, I am not talking about stretch goals. I am talking about goals and expectations that defy the logic and capability of people or process. There is a difference.

Let me give you a few examples. Let's return to the problem-solving process. What can irrational expectations do to mess up your problem-solving process? Tons. I experienced this one leader who asked the team to review their problem-solving progress on a Friday. The team had just recently finished scoping the problem and had finally received the first data dump to do their initial analysis. The system was not user-friendly (imagine that) so it took longer than they had anticipated. Regardless, they were able to determine the extent of the problem as well as the first level pareto analysis.

The team presented their update in full disclosure that they were a few days later than anticipated due to the data availability. The reaction was extreme. This leader expected the team to have completed the solution of the problem. Yes, in less than four days, the leader expected the team to do the data analysis, root cause identification, solution brainstorming and selection and finally testing and implementing the solution. Folks, that is not acting with urgency, that is irrational expectations. The team was obviously dejected from the review. They started eager to move forward with their analysis and hungry to find a solution to the top problem. By the end of the meeting, they all wanted to be reassigned and to not be part of the team. One action dramatically changed the positive energy of six people into a deflated and pessimistic environment to work in. All from irrational expectations.

I wish I could say that this was the first time I experienced this. But it was not. I have seen the same type of behavior in nearly every company I have work for. The drive to push the team to act quickly puts them up against the very process that the company is teaching them in training classes. A second example; I had a team that had completed their root cause identification. They had narrowed the root causes down to three main issues. Their analysis was solid, and they had great evidence and data supporting all three root causes. They also completed one of the best idea generation sessions I ever attended and had a list of 37 possible solutions. The solutions varied in impact, complexity, and implementation timelines. The team did a good job prioritizing them with a simple Ease/Impact matrix and were preparing to determine which solution to implement.

This is when they reported out to the senior leader. As expected, the leader spent next to no time allowing them to review the way they walked through the process. He did not ask one question about any obstacles they encountered or if there was any help they needed to move forward. He let them give a three-minute introduction of the problem and interrupted them with his first and only question; Will you be able to meet the original deadline and have the fixed by next Tuesday? The fact that no one had ever heard of the "original deadline" was bad enough. His reaction to the query of where the deadline was worse. He actually said that it didn't matter where it came from, he just needed the team to meet it or else there would be consequences. With that, he left the room.

Needless to say, the team was more than a little surprised and very anxious after the meeting. The next decision is exactly why you should not deliver illogical ultimatums within a problem-solving process. The team quickly went to their Ease/Impact matrix and had a five-minute discussion as to what could be done immediately and that is the solution they selected. They spent the next three days implementing the solution and were ready to present the outcome to the same senior leader the following Tuesday as requested. The presentation went ok, and the team was dismissed and adjourned. Job complete. Check box ticked and problem solved. I wish that were the case. Yes, the team was dismissed and adjourned, but the problem was far from solved.

In the end, the solution that was implemented was only a containment measure. It was a manual quality check to prevent field escapes to the customer. In other words, it was additional work, which translated to additional cost. Well, that is the way it started off, shortly after, the same senior leader shot down the additional labor and required the team to implement the manual check with existing team members. The problem-solving process ended up requiring more work for the team and provided zero reduction to the root causes.

The team continued to have to deal with the same amount of quality errors and they had to put more work into the process. It might shock you, but the team was not happy. The common opinion was that they would never do anymore problem solving since it just added work and leadership never cares to hear what is required to do the process. All they want is instant fixes. In about five minutes, the leader ruined his whole problem-solving process and totally killed any enthusiasm the team had for lean.

Irrational expectations do not only affect the problem-solving process. I have seen it numerous times when it comes to goal setting. Many companies go through some type of goal setting on an annual basis. The process is done a little different in most places, but the general aim is to take the high-level goals for the company and cascade them to the process level through a deployment process. Goals can be tricky, and I recommend you spend as much time deciding how to cascade them as you do developing them. It is not a simple copy and paste activity. You need to fully understand the process roll up to each high-level metric in order to determine when and who to cascade the goal to. The lean team should have a good view of the results measures (typical high-level company goals) and the related process measures. Start there.

Once you do have the appropriate target set, I suggest you provide a phased in approach to reaching the goal. Just like the problem solving that takes time, process improvement takes time, and the team should be afforded the appropriate amount of time to complete the work. What does this process cause when done with irrational expectations? Let me give an example. I worked with one team at reducing past due accounts receivables (AR). The team was given a target to reduce the past due AR from X% down to Y%. This was a reasonable target. The team did the appropriate value steam mapping activity of the end-to-end process and identified several key areas to investigate and find way to improve the associated processes. They even developed a 3, 6 and 9-month plan to deliver the improvement activity. The team then started to work on the improvement activity.

One month into their work they were asked for an update from the senior leader. The team pulled together an extensive overview of the activity planned as well as a forecast for the improvement in each of the agreed to performance measures. Things were going well until they showed the current performance chart. The team accurately showed the trend chart for the performance and the current measure was higher than the month prior. The senior leader demanded to know why they were higher than the month prior and wanted to know what they were doing to meet the target. So, we are in the first month of an action plan that spans nine months and the team had not completed any activity yet. And the leader wanted an explanation of why the performance went up in that month and what they were doing about it.

Sometimes I wonder if senior leaders even pay attention to planning activity. Newton's 1st law of Physics says, "an object in motion will stay in motion until acted upon by another object". I say this applies to process performance. Meaning, a process will continue to perform in the same trending pattern until it is acted upon with some changing process activity. So, why would any leader think the performance is going to get better if the team has not done any activity yet?! In my example, the team immediately shut down. They all but threw in the towel. They had spent a significant amount of time doing all the right things to identify the gaps and to develop the plan for improvement.

In the very first review, the senior leader crushed all their optimism and zest for learning lean process improvement. She killed the progress with irrational expectations, and she laid the groundwork for even more frustration down the road. The team tried to get back on their optimistic path, but they were constantly met with the same type of expectations. Daily management, problem solving, dashboards, standard work, process audits; everything was never done according to the leaders' timetables and they always spent three times as much time re-doing the activity. In the end, the work took months longer than it should have and the results never improved dramatically. What started off as an exciting hoshin program was dwindled into a body of work that no one wanted to participate in and around 33% of the team members left the company on their own. Irrational expectations are lean killers, and they are the ultimate in the way of disrespect. Stretch the team to think differently. Do not insult them with illogical targets.

#8 Doing the Same Ole Same Ole with a splash of Lean

I stated that allowing senior leaders to stay in their positions too long is one of the top five lean killers. This topic is related. These are some actions that are common for people trying to portray themselves as lean supporters or those who are out sailing like my favorite movie character Bob. To help you spot the Bob sailors in your organization, here are few things to look out for.

First, the Gemba walk before or after the three-hour conference room meeting. Gemba walks are the way to verify if your current state is meeting the customer's expectations from a people, process, and systems standpoint. It is the way lean leaders evaluate performance. And it IS the evaluation. In companies learning lean, the leaders are encouraged to do Gemba walks as a way to see the work and engage the team members instead of sitting in the conference room during their whole visit to the site. Those that are truly trying to learn the new way of leading, will spend a significant amount of time on the walks and they will try to replace their conference room agenda with stops in the Gemba. Production boards, inventory points, audit boards, first pass yield stations and other area provide visual status of current state performance. Attending some of the huddles and other tiered accountability meetings also provide an opportunity to observe the culture.

All and all, this person is trying to learn the new way of working. On the other hand, you have the person who follows his standard three-hour PowerPoint review in the big room with coffee, tea and snacks followed by a brief stroll thru the plant/site to wave and act interested before they hurry out to catch their flight. These are the people you need to find – and coach. A Gemba walk does not have to be perfect the first time but it needs to be a sincere attempt to be different that the traditional process.

Next is the manager who simply moves their team meeting from the conference room to the daily management board. They are harder to spot because they appear to be doing the right thing. They have a board, and they are reviewing the information with the team. These require a deeper observation from you. You need to attend one of the meetings. Does the manager simply read the slides as they did in the conference room? Does she ask anyone to help with the discussion? Does the discussion provide the team members to highlight problems that make their job hard? Is there any problem-solving activity going on? In short, is the manager just reporting the news in front of the board instead of from the conference room chair?

Another great example is the leader who always finds a way to shortchange the problem-solving process by directing the team what to do. They refuse to let the team solve the problem; they just continue in their habit of directing action. Direct and push harder is their go to action and this could not be farther from the actions of a lean leader. You are allowing these people to water down your lean efforts and you are actually making the people more sour by the day. They are forced to go to training after training and they are forced to listen to all the acronyms and fancy Japanese words from the leadership team, but they never see any of that same leadership team do anything different. In short, they read that lean is for everyone except leaders. They will support the lean effort with the equal amount of enthusiasm, and you will not see the true benefits that a lean culture can produce.

The leader left alone to continue doing the same thing they have always done is a cancer in your organization. As I said earlier, they deserve the respect to learn and grow just like everyone else. What they do not deserve, and what they should not be given, is the leeway to talk the talk and walk the same old walk. You need to act and you need to make sure the team understands why you took action. My adaption to the Navy saying I mentioned earlier is simple; On the strength on one link in the cable dependeth the might of the chain, the leader's role in the journey is to remove the weak link to strengthen the chain.

#9 Insufficient coaching resources

Let me first say that I am not a big proponent of starting your lean journey by hiring a bunch of Green Belts or Black Belts who are tasked with doing lean projects to drive cost savings. The idea of providing a surge of capacity by dedicated resources is a good approach but it needs to be a balanced approach. Meaning, it should only be used as the catalyst to spring the lean action into motion. The resources should not be considered permanent and there should be a specific plan on when to maintain and reduce them in the future. Why? Because if you have these team members in place, the rest of the team will consider it the Black Belts and Green Belts responsibility to do lean. They will not consider themselves part of the change. This will provide a void in your efforts and it will prolong the maturity curve exponentially.

Back to coaching. Coaching is the new leadership trait. It replaces directing and telling. This takes time and it takes practice. And it takes coaching from a person who has already gained the experience. Requiring a leader to change by themselves is not respectful and it is not effective. No one ever changed into something different just by being told to. They need guidance and they need someone with experience to learn from. You must invest in these resources upfront to build up the momentum. I suggest transitioning some of the Black Belt resources into coaches as the journey moves forward. The numbers can fluctuate down, and they can provide as much impact to the business by coaching the team on the tools and the culture. With that said, I also suggest that you hire some experienced coaches to help drive the learning on the tools of lean; Kaizen events, daily management, problem solving, pareto analysis, value stream mapping, transformation planning etc etc. All of these are new tools, and all of these tools can be a double edged sword if you are not careful. Let me explain.

Daily management is a foundational tool for a lean operating system. It is a process. With every process, you need to learn it in order to become effective and efficient with it. A leader and a team who have never participated in a daily management process will never be able to get good at it simply by attending a one- or two-day class. It will not happen. They need to have direct coaching on a routine basis to get better each week. This means you need to have a coach who is dedicated to be there for them. I am not saying that you need one for one coach to leader ratio in your site. I am saying that each leader/team needs to have a go-to coach who is available to support their growth. Leaving the team on their own is disrespectful. On top of the disrespect, they could waste a great deal of time and energy trying to learn on their own. This can be frustrating and, worse yet, it can be contradictory to the goal of the organization. Meaning, they can learn the wrong way of doing daily management and thus they can go backwards. Do not put them in this position. Give them a coach and allow them to learn the right way to do daily management.

Kaizen events are the engine of process improvement. When done right, they can raise the level of process performance significantly. Kaizen events are also much different from typical process improvement work in the traditional culture. In order to be different, you need to have people who understand the process of kaizen in order to execute it properly. Allowing people to carry out the old process under a new name is a waste of effort and a hindrance to your lean efforts. What that looks like is a kaizen event that ends with a laundry list of activity that must be completed to test out an idea the team came up with during the kaizen event. This is NOT a kaizen event. A kaizen event is an action event. It is one that identifies, test and implements the solution DURING THE EVENT. That is the difference. You need experienced coaches in place to help facilitate these events. Besides the poor results from the events, you can also get a sarcastic opinion of the events which can be a self-induced obstacle that you will have to overcome. One that will dampen the enthusiasm for the process as well as hinder the progress towards learning the process.

  I once had a team that was working hard to incorporate the lean fundamentals in their site. They were doing all the right things; training, developing standard work, doing value stream mapping and ensuring that daily management and problem-solving skills were being worked on by the whole. Like I said, they were doing the right stuff. Then they made the decision to do organize a kaizen event. They began preparing and reported out their intent during a leadership update. That is when they were told that kaizen events were a waste of time and they needed to do problem solving instead. Say what? A senior leader in a company who is supposedly doing lean just told the entire organization that kaizen events are a waste of time.

Needless to say, the team was shocked but quickly erased kaizen from their vocabulary. They even went out of their away to avoid the possibility of a kaizen event. One comment crushed months of progress and prevented the team from maturing their process improvement work. What a shame. This is a compounding negative affect of having a lack of coaching resources.

I already spoke a few times about problem solving. I will not go deeper but I do want to make sure you consider having sufficient resources trained and experienced to support problem solving in your organization. You should consider daily management and problem solving as one in the same. Meaning, the same coach should coach both daily management and problem solving since the two processes are co-mingled. The problem-solving process fits best as part of the daily management process. Having the same coach helps with consistency and with process knowledge and experience. In the end, you will make great strides in both at the same time.

The last place where a deficiency in coaching resources will hurt you is in the goal deployment process. Goal deployment is usually a process that comes around a few years into a lean journey. Sure, there is some strategy work being planned out in the very early stages of the effort but when I say goal deployment, I am referring to the annual alignment process that ensures all functions/business units are aligned with the corporate goals. Typically, this does not start to happen until each function and/or business unit gets a few cycles of personal improvement under their belts.

Goal deployment is a critical process and one that could result in a significant amount of work for the team. To ensure the work is developed appropriately, I highly encourage you to have ample coaching for the team in this process. Left on their own they could develop non-value-added work and they might not even be aligned to the corporate goals and objectives. I am not saying that people do not understand goals and objectives, I am just saying that there is a very fine line between functional goals and corporate goals and there is a very fine line between supporting the organization and carrying out the purpose of your function. These lines can easily be blurred and if the team is left with no coaching support, they could end up with a plan of action that could detract from their ability to support the corporates top initiatives. This would be a bad situation and it is all avoidable with the proper coaching resources in place.

#10 Combining Run the Business with Transform the Business

This is another common mistake that senior leaders make, and it is one that leads to overburdened resources and a failure to maintain stable and predictable process performance. Let me explain the difference between these two before I go further. Run the business is the equivalent to current state. It is performing our processes in the manner that we know today to meet the current customer expectations. This involves standard work, daily management, problem-solving and kaizen activity. It also requires coaching resources as well as the leaders and team members responsible for the current state performance. Transform the business is about transforming the current state into a totally different future state. It typically involves value stream mapping, transformation planning and execution as well as routine milestone assessments. It also requires coaching resources AS WELL AS resources dedicated to supporting the transformation activity which will include kaizen events, projects, and quick action activity (sometimes referred to a Just Do It activity). As you can read, both require time and resource to do it right.

All too often I see leaders engage in the transform the business with the strong desire to transform it fast. They want near instant transformation. I am not going to repeat my comments on irrational expectations, but I am going to walk down the line of resources. I have seen first-hand how successful this type of transformation activity can be when you have a dedicated team assigned to it. The team can be dedicated to the activity but not 100% of the time. Meaning, they can provide 10-20% of their time to support the transformation activity. This is very fair considering that transformation activity usually spans several months and there is not an activity planned for every single week.

Where I have seen it successful, the activity was usually part of a bigger scope called a value stream analysis. This is a strategic process and it highly effective in developing and executing lean transformation plans. If you would like to learn more about this process, I strongly recommend reading a book called "Leading the Lean Enterprise Transformation" by George Koenigsaecker. I do not get any kick back from George so it is just my free opinion.

Since I covered the good, now I will cover the bad. The bad exists when leadership expects the same coaches, leaders and team members involved with running the business to be the same people doing all the transformation activity. In short, they want a two for one payback. This is extremely disrespectful, and it is completely irrational in my opinion. Well, not just my opinion, the opinion of many people in the lean world would consider this irrational. This shows a complete misunderstanding of the two aspects of the lean operating system and it will result in a slew of negative effects for the business.

First, this will totally burn out the team members involved. They will be able to withstand a few weeks of the effort, but they will soon start to wear down and show signs of exhaustion. The signs may be subtle at first; a delay in meeting a few deadlines, inattention to detail and unplanned absences. These will become more common and they will start to dramatically impact the transformation plan. Not only will the plan start to stretch out, the amount of impact that was expected from the activity will also be diminished. This will be due to ineffective problems solving as well as poorly planned improvement activity. The team will be doing the activity; it will just take longer and not deliver the expected results. Both are not good.

A second negative affect will be ignoring the run the business work. The transformation activity will take priority and thus the run the business processes will take back seat. Remember, run the business involves current state processes deliver to current customer expectations. Failing to perform these activities is a critical risk since they are the customer facing processes. It is clear to see how the decision to utilize the same resources is directly affecting our customer experience and putting current sales at risk due to poor performance or worse.

The final affects I will discuss is the most important one, the effect on the people. Yes, the people will suffer immensely in this situation. They will not always show it at the beginning, but it will start to expose itself to an experienced observer. Lean is about respect for people. This is totally the opposite. There is a reason that we separate the work. The main reason is that it is different work and should be done by different people. Each body of work is above and beyond the normal team members role. So, both are somewhat additional in nature. To double down on that is not fair and it will overburden them to a point of exhaustion. Team members will lose energy, they will start to make mistakes and they will fail to learn anything except how to just make it through the next planned activity. They will just be going through the motions because that is all the energy, they will be able to produce.

Over time, they will make decisions to find a way out. Attrition will rise and your transformation efforts will continue to suffer. Your plan will take even longer, and the impact will be even less. This is reality and this is a direct result of your misunderstanding of the differences between run the business and transform the business. The sad part is that the leaders are seldom the ones who pay the price for their failure. The failures always seem to fall on the team members. Missing deadlines and lessened impacts are typically blamed on team performance.

The decline in current performance is usually attributed to the team taking their eyes off the ball and ignoring their responsibilities. And attrition is almost always written off as the person not being the right fit for the role. The team members suffer, and the leader keeps on pushing them harder to do the impossible, all due to their own misunderstanding. As I said, I have seen this too often and I can assure you that the team makes every effort to raise the andon, it just seems that leaders always find a way to turn the andon back on the team and ask them to reflect on what they should do differently. It is an interesting scenario. Interesting and disrespectful.

This rounds out the top ten killers to your lean efforts. I could continue the list for a few more but I want you to digest these first. Especially the first five. They are the most impactful in my opinion and they are the ones that often escape the discussions. Make no mistake about it, lean does not kill itself. Leaders do. I hope I have given you a few points to reflect on and I sincerely hope you decide to act on more than a few of them in your lean efforts. Your business will be better off for it and, more importantly, so will your team members.

8 - Meet Will Wilberscheid

Will Wilberscheid is a certified Lean Six Sigma Black Belt and certified Lean Practitioner who has successfully led enterprise-wide DMAIC projects and Lean transformations designed to reduce call center handle-time, new-hire ramp to proficiency time, and most recently, to reduce Past-Due Accounts Receivables for the North Americas. He also was part of transformation that took a 500-seat phone remanufacturing repair center from batch and queue to single piece flow which reduced cycle time from seven days to less than one hour.

Will is a former US Army Combat Medic (91B) stayed active in the veteran community after military service and works to connect veterans to corporations to find meaningful employment. And to help them overcome unconscious (and conscious) bias faced by veterans in almost every industry which causes chronic under or unemployment.

At Philips Will serves as one of the leads of the newly formed Veteran Employee Resource Group. He also served as the president of the Asurion Veteran Service group with more than 800 members nationwide.

He is an enthusiastic cyclist and never misses a Tour de France. Vive le tour! And is an avid reader who loves to learn big new ideas. He is also a passionate follower of Dave Ramsey and "Total Money Makeover" and is amazed by how much he earns when he doesn't give half the money away in interest.

Favorite book: "Extreme Ownership", by Jocko Willink and Leif Babin.

Favorite movie: Toss-up between "Good Will Hunting" (still) and "Moneyball" (using statistics to hack the world of professional baseball is just cool)

Favorite quote: "Even a lousy system beats no system every time". *Author unknown*

www.ingramcontent.com/pod-product-compliance
Lightning Source LLC
Chambersburg PA
CBHW030448220526
45464CB00006B/2452